FROM YOUNGSTERS

TO YUNGSTARS

AARON J. SMITH

FROM YOUNGSTERS TO YUNGSTARS

by Aaron J. Smith

Published by One Faith Publishing

Richmond, VA, Port Huron, MI

onefaithpublishings@gmail.com

TABLE OF CONTENTS

Day 1

IT'S YOUR LIFE

Oh, snap! You decided to open this book. Well, since you did, let's change you from a **youngster** into a **YUNGSTAR**. Shine bright young man, shine bright!

So, you know when you shining people see ya right? So, think about the lamp and how it works. Ok, the parts? You got the base and vase, the socket, and the harp.

Ok, that's the foundation.

Now for the lamp to actually work, you have to first find a bulb and plug it in. So, if you do those things the light will work, but the lamp doesn't illuminate the whole room properly… you will also need a shade.

Now, let me explain how this ties in with you **YUNGSTAR** …. Feel me?

So, the lamp basically is you. The base and vase are determined by your genetic makeup… so you know color and hair type, body type…the basics…**lol.** Then, the socket part is like how you were raised.

Some of y'all grew up in church, playing sports, family functions, and all that. Some of y'all grew up hard… jack. Family all the way turned up… I can dig it; you know how it be… different strokes for different folks. Still no excuses, won't stop - can't stop. Feel me? Sometimes you gotta get it out the mud. No other option but to win in this game called LIFE …**YUNGSTAR.**

It's your life, and no one can live it for you. If you gonna *talk* it, you need to *walk* it. (Migos) Just some real man shit. The bulb, it's your bankroll, bread, loot, and shumoney, it's what gives the lamp purpose. Go to any hardware store and look at the light bulbs, Bruh. They got many options, and that's real life as well.

YUNGSTAR, you have many options and paths to choose from to climb up the mountain of success. Remember, everyone's path is their own individual path. So, no copying the next man. Be original **YUNGSTAR.**

Key example, look at the late great Kobe Bryant. He studied MJ the Goat and implemented some of his skill set. But he then put his own sauce on it and the rest is history. There are blueprints that can be followed to get you up the mountain, the only thing is - your weather conditions are gonna be different than whoever you follow. So, be prepared!

Back to the hardware store, the bulbs have all different shapes, quality, hours that they last, etc. That's like saying lawyer, teacher, hustler, bum... all I'm saying is there's levels to this shit **YUNGSTAR**. So, level up!!

Now you got the bulb and it's time to plug in. Ok, now you got the juice you activated, and people see ya now, **YUNGSTAR** handling his business.

Y'all be wondering why all the rap artists wear shades on stage. WHY? Cause the lights shine bright, Jack, so you gots to have your shades. Same thing with the *lamp and life*. You gots to have your shades **YUNGSTAR**, 'cause if you don't, y'all get blinded by the light...Game Over!

You probably think... like damn, all this from just a lamp. **lol**... Yea **YUNGSTAR** and it ain't over yet.

What did your momma say when you leave any room in the house? Boy, turn them lights off...**lol**! I know I've been slapped for leaving the lights on. But why is it such a big deal? Lights need juice (electricity) and to have juice you must pay. So, the *'pay* to *play'* concept in life is all around. Get use to that! **lol**

Juices in life are like sacrifices. What are you willing to do to make it up the mountain? Now, some suckers might want to rob and jack (Kodak black) I get it, I can respect it. Not my way; but it's a way. **lol**

Quick money, scamming, jamming, stealing (leave that to the girls). Real men don't run in stores stealing and swiping cards and shit. Now bums and dope fiends they don't count and don't forget the feds can trace all that shit; plus, y'all on cameras.

So, it's dumb, dumb, dumb. So, now you asking, damn Love, what should I do? Now all I can say is...do you man, and stand behind everything you do, Jack.

Now everyone's moral circumference is different. So, what you're willing to do, or not do, is You. **Lol**

Remember that and stand behind your actions!

YUNGSTAR QUESTIONS

1. It's your life, and no one can live it for you, except _____
_____?

2. Life has many _____?

3. What are you willing to do to make it up the mountain? ___
_____

4. Real men don't? _____

5. Everyone's moral circumference is different. So, what are you willing to do and not do to be different? _____
_____

It's your time to shine, Yungstar!

What knowledge did you get from Day 1?

_____
_____
_____
_____
_____
_____
_____
_____
_____
_____
_____
_____
_____
_____
_____
_____
_____
_____
_____
_____
_____
_____

Day 2

RESPECT

What's up, you ready to get some knowledge you can't get in college, **YUNGSTAR?** A very important move in your life is the choice of friends you choose. You are who you hang with 'cause birds of a feather flock together.

So, while you're choosing friends, have some type of standard. I don't care how y'all moving out there, player… you gotta have a standard. Having standards is like quality control.

Like I said there's a level to this shit. Even in friendships there are levels. You have to be real with every one of them, but you gotta understand what the friendship is.

For instance, there's a crew I know that been hanging since middle school. Now they're 30 years deep in friendship. Tell me how this works… I'll sum it up with one word **"RESPECT"**

Respect is major in your life **YUNGSTAR.** Without it you'll get nowhere, and I'm not talking the street type of respect, although a little of that is needed so you won't get Chumped out here. I'm talking about letting people just be themselves…Period. When they say they're not down, and they are not ready for what you wanna do, just respect it. That doesn't mean they don't fuck with you, they're just not what you're on. That's it, nothing personal. So, respect it.

Of course, like every crew, y'all have y'all fist fights here and there. That too is part of growing up and building courage to face the world. Still, relationships continue to build afterwards. Middle and high school years are supposed to be fun, like playing sports and learning how to court girls.

You know, like having contests on who can get the most telephone numbers from girls at the State Fair. There wasn't any internet action like what y'all got now; so, you couldn't just sit at home and meet girls.

Wow! how times have changed *YUNGSTAR.*

Y'all little dudes got it easy really. Booty on duty 24/7, and don't even have to talk to the parents. That makes me laugh, 'cause charming parents was the key to even getting to talk to the girl since you had to call her home line to speak.

But what that taught you was how to respect adults and talk to them like you got some type of sense. Couldn't ask to speak to Keisha like this. "Yea, what it do Keisha moms, put Keisha on the phone"…sounds crazy right? You had to say something like this. "Good afternoon, Mrs. Campbell, is Keisha available to talk?"

It's the same thing in life, knowing what circle you're in at any moment.

When someone of authority comes into your presence how hard is it really to straighten up? That doesn't mean you're being fake. It's like this, you gotta be able to go from the crack house to the White House. You understand, G?

Be able to conduct yourself in proper form in each setting. Now, some folks will be fortunate enough in life never to be in a low-poverty situation. But, for most urban youth, you'll have a friend, cousin, and grandmother for example that lives in what white folks call the inner city (in homes which they're trying to buy back by the way).

Ok, so understanding how to move around the inner city is crucial. You can be exposed to consequences resulting in death, prison, or other byproducts of systemic racism. Moving around the White House is just as crucial; or even more so.

When speaking of the White House, I'm speaking of corporate America. What makes it more critical than anything is that you'll need credit to live a lifestyle y'all enjoy. So, learn about it ASAP.

I'm not saying you have to work for corporate America *YUNGSTAR* but Bossin' up and being an entrepreneur is definitely where it's at. It's not easy by all means.

Good Luck! See ya at the Tippy Top.

YUNGSTAR QUESTIONS

1. You must have _____

_____when choosing your friends.

2. Choosing the right friends is _____

_____

3. You gotta let people be _____

_____

4. What is major in your life, and without it you'll get nowhere?

_____

_____

5. Bossin up and becoming an entrepreneur is _____

_____

It's your time to shine, Yungstar!

What did you learn from Day 2?

_____

_____

_____

_____

_____

_____

_____

_____

_____

_____

_____

_____

_____

_____

_____

_____

_____

_____

_____

_____

_____

_____

_____

_____

Day 3

KEEP FLAVORING

YA SAUCE

One thing for *certain,* two things for *sure,* **YUNGSTAR,** money doesn't give you class. You say, what he means by that? Listen up, then I'm gonna tell ya. You little niggas don't really realize how far back black folks go with dignity and class. Even when we were slaves, we had dignity and class.

Google some old pictures of black folks. You'll see black folks booted and suited. Believe me, they were hurting financially and still had dignity and class. Feel me? Y'all might use swag or drip to explain dignity and class.

Play'a, get your sauce together. When you fix them noodles, you put that seasoning on it, don't you? Maybe some hot sauce with Fritos. Let me stop…just saying. Can't be eating them basic, with no flavor on them joints, then mix it up a little. Taste good, don't it?

Same thing in life, you gotta continue to mix it up. Keep flavoring your sauce boss. So, you'll know, high school gig, corner boy, college, vocational training, etc., etc. Them all different ingredients to make your special sauce. Remember it's your life *YUNGSTAR*… so mix it up, like them N.O. Boyz do with those gumbo flavors!!

Tell you what, I was in Washington D.C. kicking it for a friend's birthday. Whole weekend bash. During the day me and my baby were able to explore the National Museum of African Americans. It's a must *YUNGSTAR*. So, while walking through the different exhibits, and of course you can't tell our story without slavery.

We came to a concrete block. This was not just an ordinary concrete block. This particular concrete block was a block that slaves were sold off of. Think about it *YUNGSTAR*, you always hear or might even say, I love my Block. Hell, I even say it.

We've come a long way from being sold off the block, or have we? It's more folks dying on the block now than in the past, and it's by our own community. I get it and rationalize with it, cause some shit can't slide. But 97% of you can really let it ride. The consequence isn't worth it **YUNGSTAR.** Now take a deep breath, and exhale…

Keep reading and receiving this knowledge you can't get from College.

YUNGSTAR QUESTIONS

1. Money don't give you _____
_____

2. What gives you class & dignity? _____
_____

3. What caught your attention the most when you googled old pics of black folks? _____
_____

4. How are you gonna flavor yo sauce? _____
_____

5. The consequence isn't worth it **YUNGSTAR,** can you let it ride? _____
_____

It's your time to shine, Yungstar!

What knowledge did you receive from Day 3?

_____
_____
_____
_____
_____
_____
_____
_____
_____
_____
_____
_____
_____
_____
_____
_____
_____
_____
_____
_____
_____
_____
_____
_____

Day 4

MATH & MONEY

⁓

C'an't be dumb thinking you're gonna make a crumb. Math, Math, Math. How you gonna get money but don't understand basic math?

QUESTION:

How many $20 dollar bills make $500 bucks? _____

_____

Hurry up… shouldn't take long since its basic math.

The answer is 25. Twenty-five $20's makes five hundred dollars. There're several ways to get to the answer. You could've used division, or your method could be five $20s makes one hundred OR, to make five one hundreds, do 5 x 5 to equal 500. Simple right? Well, it should be. That question is just like the questions in school.

Perhaps, the question might be worded like this. Kenosha, Shawna, and Jake have a postcard collection. They each plan to put their postcards into scrapbooks to organize them.

Kenosha has 144 postcards

Shawna has 59 postcards

Jake has 98 postcards.

Shawna only wants to use 9 pages of her scrapbook.

How many postcards should she put on each page? _____

_____

How many will be left over? _____

_____

Simple solution: but, since the words were changed on ya it confused you, right?

So, what you saying, Love? Changing the verbiage makes it make sense to you.

The answer is, 6 and 5

If you're a sports person make it assists, points, rebounds, instead of postcards. Just adjust the language YUNGSTAR. Whatever you're into that's the verbiage you use. To have any type of success in life you must understand math.

For the corner boys it's a necessity to understand grams, ounces, and chemistry. So, pay attention in class. Real shit. Remember to adjust the verbiage to fit you.

QUESTION:

How many quads go into an ounce? Hurry up! _____

_____

If you don't know off the top. Stop, the corner boy lane isn't for you, Jack.

Everyone wants to be big bossin, but don't have the basics or foundation to even start…SMH.

Gotta know your shit!

Knew this White boy, Danny from one of the brokest families in the area. Always dirty, dusty, and musty…everyone used to clown on him. He was a few years younger than everyone else.

When we were getting money, it was new Jays and Maxes every other weekend, Jack. While we doing what we do, Danny would be pushing this lawn mower down the street, and it seemed like he would disappear. But quietly Danny kept getting to the money!

By time he was 16, Danny had bought a new pickup truck and trailer with a sign on that thang saying Danny's Landscape Company. Next thing you see is Danny giving boys jobs. Danny was charging folks $40 a yard. Took him 3 years to save his bread up and get his reputation high enough to be able to *really* start his own business. Goes to show, Money doesn't have an age on it **YUNGSTAR.**

Danny graduated from high school, never went to college, and now he has a landscaping company in several states. Determination, Accountability, and Standards can take you a long way in LIFE.

Danny wasn't worried about girls, popularity, or everything else youngsters are concerned with. He kept his head down, stayed focused, worked hard, and put his people on. What we used to say is, stay down to you come up.

I saw Danny's social media the other day. Just let me just say…

Dusty Danny, Salute!!!

It's your time to shine, Yungstar!

Math & Money, what new knowledge did you learn from
Day 4?

_____

_____

_____

_____

_____

_____

_____

_____

_____

_____

_____

_____

_____

_____

_____

_____

_____

_____

_____

_____

_____

_____

_____

_____

Day 5

ATTRACT SUCCESS

Aye question, did you wash your ass today, put clean socks and drawls on, and at least brushed your teeth? If so, then you got some class. If not, then you just might be a nasty ass dude...can't be having bad hygiene **YUNGSTAR**.

How you present yourself in public is key. What is perceived is received. You only get **one chance** to make a first impression. Can't be smelling and making folks run in the opposite direction. You'll never get to the money, Jack. Some of y'all need to be taught how to attract success. I just gave you the first step...hygiene that's easy.

Realizing health is wealth. Watch what you're putting in your mouth. Fast food is what it is if you can only afford fast food. But, for those that can afford a little more, go ahead and step it up a notch. Like I said, been getting to the paper from around your age YUNGSTAR.

Let me give an example. We on the block Unc says, "Nephew got a chick on deck tonight and she has her niece in town for the weekend. You trying to hang?" That's the easy button, Yelp.

So, we leave the block, hit the mall, have the dope fiends, wash the whips, split up, and go jump fly. Phone rings, its Unc, he ready, say meet him at the restaurant, chicks already there looking out the window amazed to see us pull up. Go into the restaurant and get to doing what playas do. Right?

So, peep it, the menu didn't have the prices on it. Now remember I'm your age **YUNGSTAR,** a high schooler. So, I ask the waiter how much was such and such. Why did I do that? **Lol…** cause Unc popped off.

He wasn't embarrassed, he was upset by the fact that I asked the price of food. The thing that nurture's your body, keeps everything internal working right.

He says, Fool, (that really wasn't the word by the way) we just left the mall earlier, while you were in there you never asked about a price. You were just picking up shit! So, why you playing broke? I realized then, that being able to eat good is priority number one.

24

YUNGSTAR you've seen it yourself, seeing someone with 2 racks of gear on, but playing cheap eating Mickey Dee's. Naw **YUNGSTAR** that isn't what it do.

Once again, another example that money doesn't give you class.

YUNGSTAR QUESTIONS

1. How you present yourself in public is _____

_____?

2. How many chances do you get to make a first impression?

_____

_____

3. What's the first step to attracting success? _____

_____

4. Health is _____

_____

5. Money doesn't give you _____

_____

It's your time to shine, Yungstar!

Math & Money, what new knowledge did you learn from Day 5?

_____

_____

_____

_____

_____

_____

_____

_____

_____

_____

_____

_____

_____

_____

_____

_____

_____

_____

_____

_____

_____

_____

_____

Day 6

BELIEVE IN
THE *IMPOSSIBLE*

L et me give you some news you might be able to use, **YUNGSTAR**. Peer pressure can be heavy, even worse if it's inside your household. Yea, we all know someone whose older brother or younger that's definitely hustling.

Imagine if that was your brother. What type of influence would they have on you and the decision you make in life? Most folks just do what they see. Usually, the apple doesn't fall far from the tree.

YUNGSTAR, you gotta have vision, Jack. You gotta believe in the *impossible* to be *unstoppable*. Feel me? Knew this **YUNGSTAR** grew up just like that! His big Bro was out here, getting it off the porch at the age of 12. Driving candy-painted old schools with all the accessories (rims and loud speakers) by age 14.

Just let me say, his brother had what y'all call Drip...**Lol**

Now, with all this opportunity in front of Ted to join, not only his family business but the neighborhood business. Ted had a tough choice to make. Right?

Tell you what, Ted wasn't even able to decide. Why? Family and neighborhood said NO, this isn't for you.

So instead, Ted focused on school, sports, and friendships. Did well enough being a student-athlete, that Ted was able to attend college on a scholarship offer and ended up playing professionally overseas. But those accomplishments don't compare to what's happening now.

Remember, I also included friendships. Being from the block, Ted never switched up who he ran with. Never judged his friend's decision. Let everyone do them, right? Everyone has their role in the crew, right? Realizing how much the neighborhood cheered for his success in life, Ted wanted to bless the people in his community back, and that's exactly what Ted did.

Ted ended up being a primary promoter in his city. With all that influence, Ted was able to meet and greet with powerful people. People like the Mayor, City/County Council members, Chiefs, and Lieutenants. Folks that really pull the strings and make things happen. Once he had their ear and respect, Ted **REALLY** knew he could begin to make a *BIG* difference in his community.

It took time, but you started to see small changes at first like, streetlights, and new stop signs, and then you saw the parks with new equipment, bike trails, and all. Now you know things are changing because once again, here comes a sprinkle of white people. They feel it's "safe".

Ted was researching the history about his community and found that there use to be a blacks-only beach in his neighborhood…Don't get Ted to thinking cause with Vision anything is possible!

Needless to say, Ted got a beach in his neighborhood…Salute!

YUNGSTAR QUESTIONS

1. Why do you gotta have your own vision? _____
_____

2. What about you, what's your vision, Youngstar? _____
_____

3. What you gonna do to make a difference ? _____
_____

4. How can you make a difference in your community? _____
_____
_____

It's your time to shine, Yungstar!

What new knowledge did you get from Day 6?

_____

_____

_____

_____

_____

_____

_____

_____

_____

_____

_____

_____

_____

_____

_____

_____

_____

_____

_____

_____

_____

_____

_____

_____

Day 7

WHAT'S YOUR ROUTINE?

Yea, yea, you on the *scene,* but what's your *routine?* You just out there to be out there, or are you out there making it shake? Cause there's a lot of space for losers. The winning circle is small, Jack. Not just anybody becomes a winner. You gonna have to put some work in. Mentally, spiritually, and physically. Now, all these aspects are important since they link together to make you complete.

What I gotta a problem with, is that the majority of y'all **YUNGSTARS** are weak. Not soft like a punk, but really, just physically weak. You might be in a room now with other boys your age, but my challenge is, can anyone in here drop down and give me 50 push-ups? Not them fake joints, real push-ups.

I'm a gambling man so I would put my bread down on NO. Can't none of y'all do it. That's sad, Jack. Y'all young, full of testosterone, and energy but can't push yourself up 50 times. Now ask your uncle or maybe, even your grandfather if he can. If he's a man with a physical fitness routine, I'll put my bread down on him, that he'll reach 50 push-ups.

Why? The word is ROUTINE...

When you've applied a routine to your lifestyle, consistency starts to develop. Now I'm not gonna expect you to become a full-fledged athlete. I will expect you to carry yourself with your head up, shoulders back, and chest out cause that will happen automatically if you install a physical fitness routine.

Real is Real. Face it, you're basic if you're fat and sloppy. You can be financially established, and not truly enjoy your lifestyle. Why?

First off, people talking about your image ...Real talk! You get treated differently when you're in shape, known fact...check it out! Gucci Mane is a prime example of what I'm describing. Y'all might not of know Gucci Mane in the early 2000's since y'all **YUNGSTARS**...**Google** some older pictures of him. He's gonna look like a totally different man.

Now, I'm not talking about anything other than just Gucci's physical transformation. What he was able to do was remarkably lifestyle changing. All I want y'all to do is not having to go to the Federal or state penitentiary to find time to put physical fitness into your daily lifestyle. Ya dig?

Now, it doesn't take much space to be able to perform physical fitness activities. Let me give you a simple routine to begin with every morning. If not every morning, 5 times a week. Boom, hop out the bed, yawn, shake it off, and drink a bottle of water. You up now **YUNGSTAR**. Ok, let's get it! Won't even take ya 10 minutes.

100 is the magic number for every exercise motion. **50** if you're a rookie. Break them down into sets. How many times do twenty go into one hundred? You should know, we discussed this earlier using money. Now that you know the answer, push-ups, sit-ups, and air squats are the exercises. You don't need any equipment for those. So, I don't wanna hear any excuses, **YUNGSTAR**.

Hey, you gotta go *through it* to *get to it*! So, get your body prepared for this war of LIFE.

YUNGSTAR QUESTIONS

1. What 3 aspects make you complete? _____,

_____,_____.

2. When are you starting your ROUTINE? _____

_____

3. What is your current ROUTINE? _____

_____

4. What do you need to change or add to your ROUTINE?

_____

_____

5. 100 is the magic number for every _____

_____

It's your time to shine, Yungstar!

How did Day 7 help you with your ROUTINE?

_____
_____
_____
_____
_____
_____
_____
_____
_____
_____
_____
_____
_____
_____
_____
_____
_____
_____
_____
_____
_____
_____
_____
_____
_____
_____
_____
_____

Day 8

STOP SLIPPING!

Higher than a kite…aight! Now Mary Jane is legal in most states. If you're smoking, you might as well smoke the best. But what I'm seeing youngsters doing isn't 'bout the right. Walking around looking like straight zombies like stings at night. I told them, leaning and codeing ain't gonna make you like me.

Shout out to Pimp C. R.I.P.!

Majority of y'all are popping them prescription pills. In my era we had Ecstasy. It was an upper, it made you want to have a great time at the party. Didn't make you violent. Made you hornier than anything else. So, when pussy is on your mind, you're not worrying about trying to handle the opps at that moment.

Maybe that's another reason why we didn't have as many random shootings and people dying. We weren't shooting up the club, parking lots, parks, etc. Naw, we gonna just suit up and go to where they be at, PERIOD. No innocent victims. Like earlier, you gotta have a code.

Reggie was a cat that had all the opportunities in the world at his doorstep. Went to a prestigious private Catholic High School. I mean surrounded by people that could really propel your life into quick success.

One day he decides to buy Katie from the gas station to get high. Bad move. That shit flipped his mind straight out. Ended up damn near dying after one episode. It was wild. The incident even made the local news. Since he was supposed to be someone with potential, the fact of the matter is those types of synthetic drugs gonna get you outta here.

YUNGSTAR, here's a slogan for ya... **If they gotta make it, don't take it.**

Had this youngster on the block getting a little paper ... block hugging, feel me 24/7? Only problem was he had to be 24/7 since every other night he would be nodding off frequently. Why? The little homie would be off everything. You say everything? Yes, everything!

So, while he's nodding off, boys would rape his pockets. He couldn't defend himself even though he had a firearm. Moving too slow, and he doesn't even know who did it, how it happened, or how much money he should have, I mean all dumb founded. Talking, "I ain't tripping, it's all good. Whoever did is a hoe."

Now everyone is just laughing at him. It's sad since he's choosing to play the dummy role.

He's calling the pill man every hour on the hour thinking he's winning since he's off the pills. Yes, he still had money, hoes, and clothes, but he began to look bad. Face a little rougher, hair not getting cut, you know, lacking the proper self-maintenance. We went over that earlier. Started slipping on the block, catching petty case after petty case. Making baby after baby with other trash-pill-popping thots. I mean straight loser. Can I tell you what happened to oh boy?

Now the boyz up the river. State came got 'em, slippers count, **YUNGSTAR**. Health is wealth. The drugs you take will have an effect on your body.

YUNGSTAR QUESTIONS

1. If they gotta make it, _____

_____

2. Drug will have an _____

_____ on your body?

3. Have you taken any drugs? _____

_____

4. How did drugs affect your body? _____

_____

5. Knowing what you know now, would you do drugs again?

_____

_____

It's your time to shine, Yungstar!

What did Day 8 teach you?

_____
_____
_____
_____
_____
_____
_____
_____
_____
_____
_____
_____
_____
_____
_____
_____
_____
_____
_____
_____
_____
_____
_____
_____
_____

Day 9

GET YOU SOME BALANCE!

Ain't no right way to do wrong... just try to do **wrong, right**. Now, that might sound crazy, **YUNGSTAR**. Just some Wise men's philosophy. See, you need to have balance in your life. Think about the original scale, it looks like the Libra zodiac sign. It tips in either direction, but to keep it from tipping over it takes balance and an equal amount of weight on each side. Same in life, there are positives and negatives. You must balance the two.

Let's say you punched your brother today for some reason. But you then turned around and helped your mom with some type of task. That's called balance. The negative act was punching your brother, and the positive act was you helping Mom Dukes.

Balance: Now think of something negative you did today, big, or small, and since no one's perfect, you've done something negative. It can be some negative actions you did to yourself, especially when we're supposed to be our own toughest critic.

Negative Action: Maybe you were trying to slow up buying sneakers. But some new Dunks dropped, and you had to have them, so you grabbed them.

Positive Actions: You followed up that move by selling an old pair to recoup your expense from copping the Dunks…that's **Balance**.

So, you've thought about it, do you feel like you've got balance?_____

Never thought that mumbo jumbo talk in science class really pertains to you, huh? Me neither. However, it's your lifestyle **YUNGSTAR**, keep some balance in it. Might be the difference between life or death, poverty, or riches.

Real shit, there was a robbery taking place at this trap house. At this trap they used to gamble playing Madden and 2K. Ferguson was the best around and was cleaning shop, he was just there to take some folk's money on the video game.

During the game, two armed men forced entry into the trap house, and told everyone to lay it down, which they did. It was around 12 people in the trap at the time. So, while they're running through everyone's pockets one by one, they get to Ferguson and realize they knew this **YUNGSTAR**.

He had helped one of the attacker's Grandmother for a few years with her house/ yard work. Mostly mowing, gardening, and occasionally shoveling snow from her driveway. Realizing they knew Ferguson; they told him to get out of there. Ferguson jumped up and left immediately. Ferguson's previous positive actions provided him an outlet to leave when Ferguson's friends had to stay.

Sad story, one died, 3 wounded. Ferguson never knew who the assailants were, until years later when the grandmother died. When Ferguson's mother's family friend informed her of the gratitude the grandchild showed to Ferguson on that horrific day, that made her just smile. Realizing that no matter what Ferguson was into he, he kept balance, by not letting anything steer him away from his core values.

YUNGSTAR put a positive with every negative and see **Balance** work!

YUNGSTAR QUESTIONS

1. You gotta have _____
_____ in your life.

2. What positive thing(s) did you do today? _____
_____

3. What was the reward or outcome for doing something
positive? _____
_____

4. Did you do something negative today? _____
_____

5. What is the consequence(s) behind a negative action? _____
_____
_____

It's your time to shine, Yungstar!

How did Day 9 show you how to balance your life?

_____
_____
_____
_____
_____
_____
_____
_____
_____
_____
_____
_____
_____
_____
_____
_____
_____
_____
_____
_____
_____
_____
_____
_____

Day 10

PLAN YOUR WORK & WORK YOUR PLAN

We still going in my friend. Where you been? Where you headed? So, these are questions you need to be asking yourself **YUNGSTAR**. Remember you gotta envision beyond the neighborhood. Expand, Explore, Indulge, G…

Can't have an operation without understanding the nation right, Big bossin? So, you maneuver, switch lanes, campaign, shake hands, and kiss babies.

Naw, let me slow down **YUNGSTAR**, bout to have ya'll wanting to Pimp. Hell, some of ya'll probably already sending them. While others are doing it and don't even realize it. But that's neither here nor there. You know what I'm saying. We talking about traveling, G.

Ask yourself, do I even know all 50 States? Write them down. You probably can't even do it off the top of the dome. If that's the case, catch up goofy, and Google. After that, see if you can name a city out each of the states. Write it down next to the state.

1. _____

2. _____

3. _____

4. _____

5. _____

6. _____

7. _____

8. _____

9. _____

10. _____

11. _____

12. _____

13. _____

14. _____

15. _____

16. _____

17. _____

18. _____

19. _____

20. _____

21. _____

22. _____

23. _____

24. _____

25. _____

26. _____

27. _____

28. _____

29. _____

30. _____

31. _____

32. _____

33. _____

34. _____

35. _____

36. _____

37. _____

38. _____

39. _____

40. _____

41. _____

42. _____

43. _____

44. _____

45. _____

46. _____

47. _____

48. _____

49. _____

50. _____

How many states did you know?_____

Out of those states, which ones would you want to check out? I would say all of them. WHY? Cause money is everywhere. Big cities, small cities, and towns. Opportunity is everywhere, and cultures are different across the country. What goes on in Chicago, might not fly in Miami and vice versa. But you need to get around to these cities to soak it up and implement it into your style a bit.

Like a Harlem cat, fast pacing, always racing since its 24/7 needs to have time in a small town. Where he might learn patience, which is a virtue by the way. Since things move at a slower pace. Folks don't have to rush since they don't have nothing else to do. Vice versa the small-town guy needs to see the big city so he can start his flame and begin to dream for more.

Most people I know that took their first step to exploration were people who went to college.

7 out of 10 people never came back to the city.

2 out of the 3 remaining people came back but have since left.

Leaving only 1 person who came back to live.

Now what's that saying? 9 out of 10 people who decided to explore were able to open up a door wherever they touched down. Don't be scared **YUNGSTAR**. Being scared is just part of the journey.

Nephew at the time was around 19-20, and he was working as a car mechanic; a trade that he embarked on during high school. He began feeling limited at the shop because there was such an age gap between him and the other staff. Even though he was a better employee than others his age, it held him back from promotions.

Wanting to find an occupation that age didn't matter, he became interested in the trucking industry. Nephew invested six bands to obtain his CDL license and began driving trucks for FEDEX across the country.

He was able to run a bag up and purchase a house at age 22. There wasn't a state that he didn't drive through and get paid for enjoying the view. Oh, did I mention he had to move 10 hours away for the school to learn how to operate a semi? Don't be scared **YUNGSTAR**. Salute Nephew (big bossin)

It's the same type of situation with the military. You travel, get paid, and the bonus with the military move. It's like the college lifestyle, campus, and dorms for housing and Girls, Girls, Girls, girls… I Do Adore (JAY-Z). At ten Hut. Shiiddddd… sign me up. **Lol!**

These are all decisions you must start to prepare for, **YUNGSTAR**. You must think steps ahead with your moves. Meaning you must prepare…**Plan your work and work your plan.**

All your schools, local multi-service centers, job corp, non-profit organizations, etc. have options and programs to help you accomplish these simple tasks. All you have to do is have accountable with your actions and you'll be able to bubble. NO excuses, right?

Little extra game. If you're getting out the mud, sometimes there's better soil somewhere else to plant your seed …Church.

YUNGSTAR QUESTIONS

1. Opportunity is _____
_____.

2. What is your plan? _____
_____

3. How do you plan to work your plan? _____
_____

4. You must think _____
_____ahead with your move.

5. What 's the first 3 steps to making your plan work? _____
_____

_____

It's your time to shine, Yungstar!

What did you learn on Day 10 that made you think differently?

_____
_____
_____
_____
_____
_____
_____
_____
_____
_____
_____
_____
_____
_____
_____
_____
_____
_____
_____
_____
_____
_____
_____
_____
_____
_____
_____
_____

Day 11

ME, MYSELF & I

Listen here, listen here, **YUNGSTAR**. You can't be scared to steer, ya know. Take control of your destination using an only **me, myself,** and **I** train of thought. Nothing selfish about it. You come in the world solo and leave out the world solo. Meaning, you're a **KING YUNGSTAR** so start thinking like one.

Question: What's the difference between being a good king and a great king?

Answer: Not settling,

YUNGSTAR, If you wanna be great, you gotta seek greatness!

You gotta increase your standards...

How is your kingdom going strive and survive?

How is your kingdom living?

Is it cruddy and muddy?

Or concrete floors and steel doors?

Maybe pines with plenty of sunshine?

Remember your **VISION** ... You wanna be great,
YUNGSTAR...

So, you must dream it!

KING James has a commercial out. (Side
note:)YouTube:(Thelove317; Clap Dat Powder) Nice highlights
with song, pretty cool. The commercial has Lebron grown and
Lebron as a kid. Scene is his bedroom with all the 90's and early
2000's decorations outlined with equipment for entertainment,
Nintendo, CD players, and posters on the wall, (things y'all
don't have a clue about) - no worries, it's ok. **Lol**

But he was talking back and forth with himself, and towards the
end younger Lebron asked am I ready? Older Lebron
responded, I can't tell you everything, but if you wanna make
history you gotta call your own shots. Young Lebron rebuts
with chanting, "We going to the league! We going to the
league!"

Confidence is key when calling your shots. If you don't believe, why should anyone else believe? Especially, if you're constantly fucking up. How you gonna change folks' perceptions of you? By your actions, the proof is in the pudding my Grandmother used to say. Can't trick them taste buds. You know by calling your own shots, you're demonstrating the do-it-yourself mentally, which is important as a leader.

They say to lead you must be willing to follow as well. Just another example of balance. This is why they say life's a balancing act.

What are you balancing, **YUNGSTAR**? _____

_____

Are You dotting your I's and crossing your T's?

Everyone's circumstances are different. You might be balancing school, helping your sibling, and church. Where another person might be balancing court, poverty, and homelessness. Everyone is trying to keep their life balanced in some shape or form, so we ain't judging nobody and how they gotta survive. It is, what it is!

YUNGSTAR call your own shots. Rise above any criteria, criticism, circumstance, and break them chains. There are over 300,000 more black men in college than in prison, but you wouldn't know this by watching Fox, CNN, or YouTube, would you? There are some accomplishments they've never shown. Cold world.

YUNGSTAR QUESTIONS

1. Confidence is _____

_____

2. Start thinking like a _____

_____

3. In order to lead, you must be willing to _____

_____

4. Rise above any _____,_____,

_____

5. Are there more black men in college or in prison? _____

_____

_____

It's your time to shine, Yungstar!

What did you learn on Day 11 that made you move differently?

_____

_____

_____

_____

_____

_____

_____

_____

_____

_____

_____

_____

_____

_____

_____

_____

_____

_____

_____

_____

_____

_____

_____

_____

_____

Day 12

LEARN YA HISTORY

Damn another funeral, another motherfucker
Lord knows, Lord knows, Lord knows
I smoke a blunt to take the pain out,
And if I wasn't high, I'd probably try to blow my brains out,
I'm hopeless, they shoulda killed my man as a baby
And now they got me trapped in the storm, I'm goin crazy,
Forgive me; they wanna see me in my casket and if I don't blast I'll be a
victim of them bastards.
I'm loosin' hope, they got me stressin',
Can the Lord forgive me?
Got a spirit of a thug in me
Another sip of that drink, this Hennessy got me queasy.

Don't wanna earl, young nigga take it easy.
Picture your dreams on a triple beam, and like it seems
Don't underestimate the power of a fiend
To my homies on the block
Slangin' rocks with your glocks, put this tape in your box
When you're runnin from the cops, and never look back.
If they could be black, then they would switch
Open fire on them busta-ass bitches, and
Lord knows.

~Tupac Shakur

The year was 1995, and what was going on then, is still happening now. Damn shame, we as a culture haven't developed. Who's fault? Ours, YUNGSTAR.

In 1991 Rodney King got his ass whooped in LA by 6 white policemen. Just so happens, someone had actual footage of the incident. No need to tell you how that turned out. **Google** it. Take some time out right now to research that and other disturbing incidents that have happened to our people.

When I'm conversing with most of y'all YUNGSTAR's, y'all have no clue about your history. So, please get your phone, tablets, laptops, and begin to Google. Best thing about Google is that you can type in any question. If you've done that, tell somebody you've got some news that they can use, ya dig? Spread it.

Now back to the very first eleven words of the song. Those were the ones that have the most pain behind them. Aren't you tired of having to attend another unnecessary funeral? The whole routine becomes a hassle, right?

Ain't you tired of looking at Mommas, Sisters, and Aunties crying while having to mingle with all the fake ass people only there for the show? We were going through that 30 years ago, **YUNGSTAR**. Some trends need to fade out and that's one. Change the standards, right?

Lord/Allah knows it's even deeper. Right? Gotta believe in something bigger than yourself. So, making your decisions knowing the Lord/Allah knows should have an impact on how you're handling things. The Lord/Allah forgives all men who ask for forgiveness.

The game gives you what you give it. The old cliché: live by the gun, die by the gun. Let me tell ya, that's real wisdom, **YUNGSTAR**. Listen, man… pretty much all the gun totters, jackers, robbers, and silly head dudes from my era are dead… Game Over!

YUNGSTAR QUESTIONS

1. What other disturbing incidents did you find on Google?

_____

_____

2. How can you relate to the lyrics in Tupac Shakur's song?

_____

_____

3. The Lord/Allah forgives all men who ask for _____

_____

_____

4. The game gives you _____

_____

5. Live by the gun _____

_____

It's your time to shine, Yungstar!

What did you learn on Day 12 that you didn't know yesterday?

_____
_____
_____
_____
_____
_____
_____
_____
_____
_____
_____
_____
_____
_____
_____
_____
_____
_____
_____
_____
_____
_____
_____
_____
_____

Day 13

GET YOUR DOLLARS UP!

You're worried about getting your followers up? **YUNGSTAR,** you need to get your dollars up! Drake definitely was throwing y'all some game. All you see is people with their heads down lurking on social media, all day, every day. It's really lame and pointless if you're not getting paid off it.

Yea, you might be informed with all the fake news that's on social media. Not saying real truthful information isn't, but statistics suggest it's claimed to be fake news. So, why absorb the bullshit 24/7?

You might say, what else is there to do? I laugh at some stupid questions, **YUNGSTAR**. What else, there's always something else to do. The game never stops since the world keeps spinning. You must become serious about elevating your life. So, flip that social media shit, and get to the paper with it. Doesn't make any sense if you got a following but not getting any **Shumoney**.

Find a product to sell. Something legal, for the boys that went left, FEDS remembered. Anything sells, even water. You've seen them boys in Atlanta pushing water so hard it went viral. That's what I'm saying. You can laugh at them boys all you want, but they making it happen. Ain't sitting around wasting space and catching a case. Them boys done touch hands and chop game with famous stars, ghetto celebrities, and APD.

Now that's what you call a winning circle, **YUNGSTAR**. I'm not saying duplicate what they did since that's their thing.

What's your thang is the question? _____
_____
_____

Take a minute, think about it. OK, you've got one. At least you got one since some don't. Congrats. Now ask yourself, am I really good at this thang? **YUNGSTAR**, you're your toughest critic, right?

Roll with that thang then. See how you can develop it into a stream of cash flow. Use your "social media" resources to establish clientele. I've seen **YUNGSTARS** come up with all types of businesses that are working. The sky's the limit! And yes, it's great to be a national brand, reaching across the country and selling a product or service. That's gonna take a lot of time and effort to accomplish success. Since bossin up isn't easy.

Remember white boy Danny? He was just cutting people's lawns? Simple, he had his local area on smash. So, there's always a way. Look in your neighborhood to see what it's lacking. Then try to provide that **Product** or **Service**.

Service could be as simple as carrying old folk's groceries. Sounds monkey, right? Like yo, this lame carrying groceries. Next time you see my man carrying groceries, take a good look at him. Did you peep his sneaks? They were fresh, right? **YUNGSTAR,** he doing something right. Just telling you what I know.

I watched Boogie bag groceries at the Commissary after working 4 hours, since he's still in high school. Might leave with $65-150. With vision Boogie saw the bigger picture by working there. Boogie was meeting everyone in the area working there. One thing for certain, two things for sure. Americans gonna eat. Meaning the grocery store gonna stay packed. Boogie also was just beginning to indulge in the dope game. Remember it's not **what** you do, it's **how** you do it.

Boogie continued to go to school in the day, work, and finish at night on the block. Wake up and do it all again. Game has changed a bit since the day when you actually had to stand on the corner with 10 other people that have the same product.

Why do most customers choose Boogie to do their dealings with?

———————————————————————————————

———————————————————————————————

———————————————————————————————

Familiarity…they've seen Boogie elsewhere. That gives them a different perspective of who Boogie is and what he's involved with. Hell, they shouldn't be trying to buy the shit either. Everybody's wrong and trying to do wrong the right way. The other hustlers on the block don't understand why they've got to wait until Boogie leaves to make a sale. Remind you, they all have the same exact product. Stop and think why?

Boogie's customer service was like Chick-fil-a's. Made you laugh, right? Those folks always got a smile and treat you like you've made their day for patronizing their restaurant. Makes you wanna come back for more and more.

By working for the Commissary, Boogie learned excellent people skills and used them to his advantage to bubble. Flexing three muscles on the hustle during his teenage years. School, part-time job, and block monster. Salute!

Don't want to crush any dreams, but this wasn't referring to anything tied to the entertainment industry like being a model, rapper, or singer. Social media is a platform, but there's a whole lot of other machines behind the scenes. Trust!!

Good luck, Yungstar!

YUNGSTAR QUESTIONS

1. Do you have more followers on social media or more money? _____

_____

2. If you got more followers, what can you start doing legally to get yo money? _____

_____

3. Can you provide a **PRODUCT** or a **SERVICE**? _____

_____

_____

4. How can your **PRODUCT** or a **SERVICE** help your customers? _____

_____

5. Write down 5 Plans to make your Plan work

1._____

2._____

3_____

4._____

5._____

It's your time to shine, Yungstar!

You got this, Yungstar!

_____

_____

_____

_____

_____

_____

_____

_____

_____

_____

_____

_____

_____

_____

_____

_____

_____

_____

_____

_____

_____

_____

Day 14

YOU GOTTA
HAVE STANDARDS

I got 99 problems and a Bitch ain't one, **YUNGSTAR.** Be careful who you're fucking because it might be a mistake that lasts a lifetime. First and foremost, you've heard it and heard it…wear a damn condom!

I know **YUNGSTAR,** easier said than done since that pussy be gushy. But putting that condom on eliminates 99 percent of problems that can occur.

Meaning, the baby ain't mine first off. Second, when the clinic calls asking if you've had intercourse with such and such, you immediately hit them with, "I used a condom!"

Feel's good to be stress-free when it comes to dick control. That's essentially what it is, mind over matter. Can you stop the urge to dive in raw? Oh, **boi!**

If it's too late and you've already fumbled the ball and became a father, Congrats! Fatherhood used to be what a man made it. Nowadays, these girls wanna be the mommy and daddy…period!

Since most haven't grown up with a father, they continue their own lifestyle legacy…**No Fathers Allowed Zone!**

Girls think they got pussy powers, look at all these girl rappers. All claiming to have the **WAP**. Ain't no way every girl in the world has that good good. So, stop going for the mumble jumble **YUNGSTAR**, gotta put some charisma behind your macking. All that shy boy in-person act, but when on social media you're super confident, swaggered out, and shit. What kinda sense does that make?

To qualify and be able to satisfy a top-notch chick, you gotta be keeping your standards high. Focusing on progressing yourself will automatically create an aura or *glow*. That will make the girls watch and pay attention. They need to be watching tv because watching you is like pay-per-view by the way.

It'll cost them something, you don't care if its help with schoolwork, buying extra snacks at lunch, or maybe even she gave you a pre-rolled joint for afternoon enjoyment. You gotta have **Standards**.

Treat them like they treat themselves. If she bopping and topping, then thot, thot on. If she's trying to be a decent girl, let her be a **YUNGSTAR**...Real shit.

You gotta know when to let someone grow. Remember Ted and his hood. There's gonna be a few girls that can make it out the situation they're in. Let them be. We gotta have some Queens out here, right King?

When you go over to a chick's spot, have standards, **YUNGSTAR**. If she's living with her mom, there shouldn't be any reason why the house isn't neat or tidy.

If it is multiple ladies in a household and the house isn't spotless, that's a major sign to run in the opposite direction cause the women in that household are lazy. Can't have a lazy woman, right? They scream all this teammate talk. Well, my teammates pull their own weight like they should, right?

It's not about her beauty, it's about her duty. Know this, **YUNGSTAR**. Vandero, a real balanced little nigga...daddy was a hustler, did time upstate, Mom dukes on the other hand got the plan for the brother man. Got all types of *foundations* to help folks in *situations*.

Van, growing up like most kids, had all types of buddies. They all had girls, but the girl Van chose wasn't like his buddies. Van's chick lived in the sticks. Ya'll know, real corn field type scene. Van would drive an hour every weekend to lay up with his chick. Van's buddies clowning since she happens to be a little uglier than the girls they were dealing with.

Let me tell you, them dudes ended up having babies with thots, going to jail, and a few got killed before the age of 24. Now, Van on the other hand laying low up in the boondocks, he's *maintaining* and not *complaining*.

Van got a raise on the job and headed back to school to further his career with the encouragement of the company. Still with the same girl, and they still don't have any children. Checking off all the boxes to be able to have **high standards**.

Gotta say it's impressive, Van.
Salute!

YUNGSTARS QUESTIONS

1. Putting on a condom can eliminate _____
_____of my problems.

2. To be able to satisfy a top-notch chick, you gotta _____
_____
_____

3. Progressing yourself will automatically create a _____
_____
_____

4. What does having high standards mean to you? _____
_____
_____

5. Why should you have high standards? _____
_____
_____

It's your time to shine, Yungstar!

How did Day 14 shine some light in your life?

_____
_____
_____
_____
_____
_____
_____
_____
_____
_____
_____
_____
_____
_____
_____
_____
_____
_____
_____
_____
_____
_____
_____
_____
_____

Day 15

YOU GOTTA
HAVE A MENTOR!

Do you have a mentor, **YUNSGTAR**? I ain't talking about nobody on TV either. Someone you can actually touch and soak some game from. Someone you aspire to be like in some shape, form, or fashion. Cause you gotta have someone to help you swerve some of life's potholes, cause there out there, **boi.**

A good mentor is important, they become like family since you've got to let them into your circle to fully get the best out of the situation. In life, I've personally had several mentors to guide me in whatever lane I'm sliding through at the moment.

Being financially stable has always been my main focus during this journey called life. So far, so good. I've been blessed!

There's one particular mentor that has had a lasting imprint on my train of thought. Old man Doc said to me, "It's easy to get money, the thing is can you keep it?"

Now think about what he's saying, **YUNGSTAR.**

Let me tell ya, society is set up for you to spend every dime you get, and then go into debt and spend some more money. So, holding on to the almighty dollar is hard, **YUNGSTAR**. It takes financial discipline and courage to not let peer pressure force you into spending that bag on material stuff.

Now for Doc, it was easy to get money, I mean the old man was flowing in paper. How I met Doc was crazy. It was a family trip to NYC to see the play *"Color Purple"*. I ended up meeting him during the intermission because he liked what he saw from me. Remember, people always watching. Noticing I was with my mother, grandmother, and my baby momma, I figured it showed him character.

Afterward, he invited us to dinner and the rest is history. We've been tight ever since. At the time I met DOC he was the co-club owner of one of the top nightclubs in the country. The club so big, it had a movie theater in the VIP section.

During that time, all the top stars performed there. This just a few, The Dipset Crew, T.I., P Diddy, Lil Wayne, Yo Gotti, etc. Seriously, it was a performer every weekend. The club was lit. Doc's bag was heavy just from that alone.

Let me take you back to the '70s, **YUNGSTAR**. This how long DOC has been an official. See, you never know how the things in life you've done already, can and will benefit you later in life. After college DOC joined the military.

During his enlistment, he learned how to fly airplanes, and after his time in the military, he became a college professor. That's why we call him, DOC.

While teaching and coaching at the college, a streak of luck happened. The college made it to the Final Four in men's basketball. The only issue was that the Final Four was being held in the upper Western region of the country, and both of the teams that made the championship game were located in the Midwest.

This obviously was making it a logistical problem to attend the game. The question the school board had was, how can we get the student body and fans out to the game?

DOC, always the thinking man, said to himself, "Hell, I can fly a plane". Realizing at the time, the school's location had the largest runway in the state (at the military base). DOC being a part of the administration and sports department was able to provide air travel to the championship game (for a fee of course).

DOC secured the bag by just being in the right

spot at the right time and using his platform to his advantage. He was able to solve a problem without really including too many others.

What I need you to take away from this, **YUNGSTAR** is that you'll never know that the things you're interested in now may very well help you later secure your bag.

Be open to learning all types of things, even what you might think is the silly stuff. Sometimes knowing that silly stuff can change your life and lead to opportunities you never saw coming.

Despite growing up in a small town, DOC crawled out and has guided hundreds of young men in their journey through manhood...*100*

Salute, see ya on your soul day!

YUNGSTARS QUESTION

1. A good mentor is _____

_____

_____

2. Why is a good mentor important? _____

_____

_____

3. Be _____to learning all types of things.

4. It takes _____and _____to
not let peer pressure cause you to spend all your bag on material
stuff.

5. Knowing silly stuff can change your _____

_____

_____

It's your time to shine, Yungstar!

What did you learn today that you didn't know yesterday?

_____
_____
_____
_____
_____
_____
_____
_____
_____
_____
_____
_____
_____
_____
_____
_____
_____
_____
_____
_____
_____
_____
_____
_____

Day 16

DROP THAT TIP!

If you're on the *scene,* then play it *clean.* You might ask what that means. Well, let me say this, it's about not seeing what you saw and not always hearing what you heard.

Coming from where we talk down on someone who's cooperating with authority. Authorities such as law enforcement, school administration, social workers, etc., etc. We tend to label someone of that stature a SNITCH!

Now everyone can have their own bias on what a snitch is. It's all about perspective, **YUNGSTAR**. When you've been caught in an act of crime and you're an active participant of the crime, there's no reason whatsoever to roll over and give someone up....*SNITCH*!

You made the bed, so you MUST lay in it. Now, on the other hand, if someone dragged you into a situation without your knowledge, then that's slightly different. Remember, it stems back to choices.

Take DB for example, DB was a top 5 basketball player growing up in the city. He had all types of potential, and he was selected to attend ABCD/ Nike camp during the summer which was big in those days.

During high school, DB didn't understand the importance of making good grades. You should know what that means, you've seen Netflix. Junior College here we come. DB had to attend the #1 Junior college at the time. While there he ended up getting pretty close to a teammate. DB came from an environment where everyone is doing something illegal, he wasn't concerned about his teammate's actions and decisions. But of course, that ended up backfiring.

One particular day, DB's teammate's cousin came to town. All the team players lived off campus in a huge apartment complex, where most of the college students lived. So, the complex was lit. Cuzo was in such shock to see black guys running around fucking with the white girls with no issues, so he decided to sponsor a get-together. All day, Cuzo spread the news about throwing a party and everything was on him.

Unknown to DB was the fact that Cuzo was a broke and stunning type of dude. Remember, it's his teammate's cousin. Later that afternoon they all loaded into a car and headed to get some chicken for the party. Back at this time, there wasn't a Wing Stop or Jordan's type of spot to go grab chicken. The vehicle happened to be a two-door; DB is in the back behind the driver seat sitting long ways. His teammate's cousin is the driver. On the way there, they hotbox the car. Basically, they smoked a blunt on the way.

As they pulled into the lot and parked at the Church's Chicken location, DB stays in the backseat as his teammate and teammate's cousin go into the Church's Chicken. While inside, Cuzo decides to rob the damn store. What the fuck was he thinking! DB noticed what was occurring, now he was in motion trying to get out of the back seat of the two-door car. DB wasn't able to get out of the car before they jumped back into the car and sped off!

They made it back to the complex, DB is extremely pissed and arguing with the others. They get inside the apartment, and it wasn't even five minutes before the police were there and arresting everyone. DB gets down to the station and the police begin the interview. The first question from the detective's mouth was, "Tell us your side of what happened?"

Question: What would be your response in that situation? ___

_____

_____

Now, this is DB's teammate and teammate's cousin. So, really how loyal should he truly be?

Let me tell you what DB said, "I want an attorney". DB stood tall knowing he truly had nothing to do with the incident. So, with an attorney and everyone else being real nigga's, DB was able to finish the basketball season and school year.

The other's got time, **YUNGSTAR**. Armed robbery isn't a lightweight case. Feel me? But them boys took their time on the chin like a G, and they told the judge that DB had no clue what was going to occur. Leaving the Judge no other choice but dismiss the case against DB.

Now some of ya'll might have said I would've just told what happened. Yes, there's nothing wrong with telling the truth. I'll never say not to tell *your* truth. DB was just fortunate enough that he was with the right type of individuals that had character enough to take their case like you should. Everyone isn't a stand-up cat. Be careful who you're doing dirt with.

Rule of thumb, **YUNGSTAR**…women, and kids are off limits. If you witness something or hear about anything happening fucked up to a child or woman, unless the woman is actively living that lifestyle, then she's fair game. Gotta add the elderly men too. Can't be letting anything happen to deacon Johnson. Feel me? **lol**

Go ahead and drop that tip, **YUNGSTAR**. Real shit! Might be someone you love one day that you'll need someone to step up and say something.

YUNGSTAR QUESTIONS

1. Have you ever been in a situation where you had to snitch?
_____
_____

2. What did you learn from DB's story? _____
_____
_____

3. What could DB have done differently to avoid that type of
situation? _____
_____

4. Children, women, and elderly men are _____
_____
_____

5. Be careful with who you doing _____
with.

It's your time to shine, Yungstar!

Can you relate to anything from Day 16?

_____

_____

_____

_____

_____

_____

_____

_____

_____

_____

_____

_____

_____

_____

_____

_____

_____

_____

_____

_____

_____

_____

_____

_____

_____

Day 17

TIME DOESN'T
WAIT ON NOBODY!

The day you *lay off* is the day it doesn't *pay off!* Believe it, **YUNGSTAR**. Wait for what, since time waits for no man? So, you might as well get moving. Stick and *move* to the *groove,* understand me?

I overheard a conversation between an OG and an 18-year-old.

He asked **YUNGSTAR** what type of training or career he wanted to pursue. He said, "Well sir, I would like to become an engineer. But it requires much training and I'm afraid I would be too old when I finish."

The OG sat in silence for a moment, then laughed and asked, "**YUNGSTAR,** how long would it take to become a successful engineer?

"Seven years or so" he replied.

"How old would you be afterward?"

YUNGSTAR responds, "twenty-five"

Then, OG asked." How old will you be in seven years if don't become an engineer?"

"25 I guess"

Moral to the story is time waits for no one, **YUNGSTAR.**

So, don't hesitate to make your moves. Plan your work and work your plan. Don't let life distract you from completing your tasks, goals, and missions. Successful folks don't let the pitfalls take them out the game. They find solutions to the problems and keep pushing.

While simps complain, make excuses, and soak in their misery. **YUNGSTAR,** don't become one of those people that always have a sad story to tell. Like they're the only ones with issues. Only difference is, they let the issue become long-term. When you should handle the issue with a short-term train of thought.

All problems have a solution…period! You just have to focus and direct your attention and resources to handle it. As a

YUNGSTAR you're capable of taking responsibility for yourself. Housing should be the only issue restraining you if you're under the age of 18.

Part-time work is always around. So, you should be able to handle feeding, clothing, and entertaining yourself, solo, without help from your parents. So, whether you come from a dead-beat parent(s), or you're coming from a two-parent household, you shouldn't be dependent upon anything from your parent(s) other than housing.

Meaning…get your priorities together, **YUNGSTAR**. You can do it!!!

Remember, you won't be the first to rise from the gutter. I've told you; the blueprints are out there.

Check this quote out from Samuel Smiles. *"All work and no play makes Jack a dull boy, but all play and no work makes him something greatly worse."*

I guess hard work pays off!

YUNGSTAR QUESTIONS

1. Who does time wait on? _____

_____

_____

2. What type of career do you want to pursue? _____

_____

_____

3. How long will it take for you to finish to become successful?

_____

_____

4. Successful people find _____to their _____

_____and keep it _____

_____

5. All issues are short _____

_____,

and that means issues don't last forever.

It's your time to shine, Yungstar!

How did Day 17 help you with understanding the importance of not wasting time?

_____

_____

_____

_____

_____

_____

_____

_____

_____

_____

_____

_____

_____

_____

_____

_____

_____

_____

_____

_____

_____

_____

_____

Day 18

COWABUNGA DUDE!!

Cowabunga dude, yea on my Teenage Ninja Turtle shit! Ya'll little dudes don't know nothing about that. Naw, **YUNGSTAR** just talking. But on some real, that surfing scene is damn near like life in general. Think about the process of going to surf.

First you must muster up the courage to even decide to try. Like real life, right? Can't succeed if you don't try. Now you have to get to the beach, just like life. What route are you gonna take?

Before you hit the road you gonna need supplies: beach towels, surfing gear, and most importantly, the surfboard. Now, all of those supplies cost. So, that means you're investing into the process, just like real life again.

Now you've parked and begun walking to the water, while walking to the water you should be observing the waves and how the other surfers are handling them. Once again just like life, soak wisdom and game from other people.

Now you're ready to go try it for yourself. Take a step into the water and begin to shiver since the waters are chilling. Just like life, since it gets uncomfortable at times. But you got use to the temperature and begin to paddle out far where the waves are. While paddling, you're seeing other surfers ride waves, and seeing surfers crash out on waves. But you keep paddling strong. Like life, only the strong survive.

Now you've made it to where you feel the waves are right for you. So, you're sitting on the board and waves are coming, and you're deciding not to take them. Nothing wrong with that. Patience is a virtue; so, wait for the one you think is for you. Like life again, everything isn't for everyone.

Do your thing, **YUNGSTAR**. Now you've been out there for 30 minutes, and the sharks haven't attempted to bite at you, yet. See, the haters aren't always hating.

Here it comes, the wave you've been waiting on. You start paddling so you can hop on the board and ride this wave. Everything is going smooth, the wave comes, and you take one more stroke and jump onto the surfboard. Perfect with a secure stance! Ten toes down. The wave is now carrying you across the ocean like water itself. You're inside that wave doing your damn thing. Whatever that is. So, when I'm saying, "Cowabunga dude!" I'm really saying, **YUNGSTARS**, show up and show out on your wave!

You're inside the wave and you pop out the other side to everyone's amazement. Like life again, folks are always watching. You cruise in land, hop off the board, take a drink of water and then do what? You should say to yourself… that was fun. I'm going right back out to do it again.

Just like Life, you can't stop! Won't stop riding your waves **YUNGSTARS**.

You know what I'm thinking? The weather nice, mid 80's. Yea it's about time for me to go catch a wave. Never get too old to go catch one, **YUNGSTARS**.

Cowabunga Dude!!

YUNGSTAR QUESTIONS

1. You can't succeed if you don't _____

_____

_____

2. Do you ever feel like you're surfing on the waves of life?

_____

_____

_____

3. How do you cope with the waves in life? _____

_____

_____

4. Just like surfing those waves, I can't _____
and I won't give _____

_____

5. People are watching you, so show up and _____

_____

_____

It's your time to shine, Yungstar!

What knowledge did you receive from Day 18?

_____
_____
_____
_____
_____
_____
_____
_____
_____
_____
_____
_____
_____
_____
_____
_____
_____
_____
_____
_____
_____
_____
_____
_____

Day 19

YUNGSTARS

What's happening, Captain? Just another day to rise and grind. So, I'm on mine, are you on yours, **YUNGSTAR?**

+ Did you wash your ass this morning?
+ Did you do your physical fitness routine this morning?
+ Have you dotted your I's and crossed your T's this morning?

The answer to these questions should be yes.

Great job, **YUNGSTAR!** Now you're developing into that dude you truly want to be. It takes effort every day to see subtle changes in your life. Nothing that's worth anything comes overnight.

You see it all the time. Someone hits a lick, you know, shooting dice, robbing someone, etc., etc. and they seem to be on top for the moment. Most of the time they capping on social media like they're big dog status. See them fools 3 months later, back broke asking someone to put them on. Damn shame.

Same story that you've heard from day one. Who wins the race? The tortoise or the hare? My father (RIP) used to say, "Life is like a marathon, so slow down and pace yourself. Got a long time to compete, finish, and win the race."

You can only think like that if you plan on being in the game of life for the long haul. Half of the **YUNGSTARS** believe they won't even be around to see the young age of twenty-five. "Fuck it!" is the common word I hear from the ones who have given up and don't really know why they've given up.

I spoke with the Minster Nuri Muhammad today, (google him) while handling my physical fitness routine. He dropped a gem on me that I've got to share.

He said, "Why you think **YUNGSTARS** shoot each other so much these days?"

I responded, "Because they scared to get punched in the mouth."

Minster said, "Good point, but that's not all. See when you have conflict, issues, and disputes, you're supposed to *look up* into your mind to figure out the problem. But most people don't have anything up there to grasp on to, so, they *look down*. Which there's usually a gun on their waistline that can be grabbed."

I thought that made some sense. People with brain power can usually handle disputes without violence. So, keep soaking and implementing knowledge so you can continue to grow. That's the whole meaning behind, **YUNGSTARS**.

Y - Youngster

U - Understanding

N - Needing

G - Game

S - Starts

T - Turning

A - Around

R - Race

S - Standards

YUNGSTAR QUESTIONS

1. What does your Rise & Grind routine look like in the morning?

List 3 things that you do when you first wake up.

1. _____

2. _____

3. _____

2. What can you add or change to make your morning routine better? _____

_____

3. It takes _____

_____

to see a change in your life.

4. Anything that's worth something doesn't come _____

_____

_____

5. What does a YUNGSTAR mean to you? _____

_____

_____

It's your time to shine, Yungstar!

How did Day 19 make you feel after reading it?

_____

_____

_____

_____

_____

_____

_____

_____

_____

_____

_____

_____

_____

_____

_____

_____

_____

_____

_____

_____

_____

_____

_____

_____

_____

_____

_____

_____

Day 20

"THE GLOW"

You've made it to the last day, **YUNGSTAR**. CONGRATS!!

And they say you can't start and finish shit. What they thought? (**LOL**) But, like the words of Barry Gordon's legendary produced movie, *The Last Dragon's* soundtrack suggests, **YUNGSTAR**. You got to have the GLOW!

> **Definition of GLOW:**
>
> **VERB: give out steady light without flame**
>
> **NOUN: a steady radiance of light or heat.**

Take life one day at a time.

That's what a wise man said to me.

He said, "Life, in all its complexity

Is the ultimate test for you and me."

When you walk holding your head up high

For the Master's watching you from the sky

I know not what trouble lies ahead

Before you fight, use your head.

It's time to leave the nest where you were born

This journey you must make alone.

(Spread your wings and fly)

There's a power deep inside you, an inner strength

You'll find in time of need.

(The Glow)

Like the seasons, love will come and go

If it's right, you'll automatically know.

The world of mystery exists only in your head.

When you become one with yourself

The wall will fall

The journey now before you *is* the final test

You've learned your lesson well.

(I can teach you no more)

There's a power deep inside you, an inner strength

You'll find in time of need

(**The Glow**)

YUNGSTAR, the **Glow** can be anything you focus on accomplishing. Nobody can stop you if you apply the wisdom that is obtained from reading this book. Hey man, I believe in ya if nobody else does, **YUNGSTAR**.

Good luck in life, see ya at the top jack! You are the new generation that will have to continue to set the **Standards**. You possess the power of the **Glow, Yungstar** … Shine on, shine on.

YUNGSTAR QUESTIONS

1. Has this book made you think and move differently in life?

_____

_____

2. If so, how? _____

_____

_____

3. After reading this book, do you believe you can achieve
anything you put in your mind to do? _____

_____

_____

4. What does getting wisdom mean to you? _____

_____

_____

5. What wisdom did you get after reading this book?

List 5 wisdom nuggets you received.

1. _____

2. _____

3. _____

4. _____

5. _____

It's your time to shine, Yungstar!

_____

_____

_____

_____

_____

_____

_____

_____

_____

_____

_____

_____

_____

_____

_____

_____

_____

_____

_____

_____

_____

_____

_____

_____

_____

_____

_____

_____

_____

_____

_____

It's your time to shine, Yungstar!

It's your time to shine, Yungstar!

_____
_____
_____
_____
_____
_____
_____
_____
_____
_____
_____
_____
_____
_____
_____
_____
_____
_____
_____
_____
_____
_____
_____
_____
_____
_____

It's your time to shine, Yungstar!

It's your time to shine, Yungstar!

_____
_____
_____
_____
_____
_____
_____
_____
_____
_____
_____
_____
_____
_____
_____
_____
_____
_____
_____
_____
_____
_____
_____
_____
_____
_____
_____

SPECIAL THANKS

Special thanks to the folks that's been referenced in this testimonial book. Y'all some solid men. Proud to say, I'm a friend of many men with **high qualities** and **standards.**

SALUTE!!

Made in the USA
Monee, IL
27 September 2023

43546286R00069